BUILDING A TRUSTED EXPERT CULTURE:
Six Pillars of CRM Success

GORDON HILLEQUE
Founder of *CustomerTRAX*

Building a Trusted Expert Culture: Six Pillars of CRM Success
Copyright © 2015 by Gordon Hilleque

ALL RIGHTS RESERVED.
No part of this publication may be reproduced, stored in a retrieval system, or transmitted, in any form or by any means—electronic, mechanical, photocopying, recording, or otherwise—without prior written permission.

Ghostwriter: Carla Ewert
Design by: Jenny L. Smith

ISBN 978-0-9892910-4-0

"I believe your goal is to become the Trusted Expert customers rely on. This means taking an entirely different approach to CRM by focusing on team development in order to enhance customer relationships. It means training your team to truly understand customers' needs so that they can help customers recognize and overcome the challenges facing their businesses."

—GORDON HILLEQUE

TABLE OF CONTENTS

Introduction **9**

Driving Forces—Perceived **12**

Driving Forces—Real **19**

Cultural Barriers **24**

Adoption Sucess **31**

The Bottom Line **56**

Notes **60**

INTRODUCTION

In recent decades customer relationship management has been a pet project for many companies intent on retaining customers and increasing the bottom line. While CRM seems to be the key to staying relevant and responsive to customers, achieving long-term, company-wide adoption of a CRM product is quite difficult. **In fact, statistics say more than half of all adoptions are unsuccessful.**[1]

This reality creates a tension; CRM is vital to customer care in today's market, but CRM software can be a risky investment.

Having worked with companies at various stages of CRM implementation for almost 20 years, I believe adoption difficulties reflect a larger complexity. Indeed, companies are often missing the real issue in customer relationships.

I wrote my first booklet, *Trusted Expert Formation: Re-envisioning Your Approach to CRM*, to help companies rethink traditional customer relationship management and draft a vision statement that aligns with specific company goals.

In it, I suggest that traditional CRM needs to be completely re-envisioned. The very term customer relationship management implies that customers are a problem to solve and the goal is to find ways to ease the burden they create. But customers don't want to be managed, and approaching them as data that benefits your company will do little to improve customer experience and increase loyalty.

Instead, I believe your goal is to become the Trusted Expert customers rely on. This means taking an entirely different approach to CRM by focusing on team development in order to enhance customer relationships. It means training your team to truly understand customers' needs so that they can help customers recognize and overcome the challenges facing their businesses.

Trusted Expert Formation: Re-envisioning Your Approach to CRM helps identify questions to ask and tools to use to craft a vision statement that will put you on your way to becoming a Trusted Expert. Once you have that vision statement, how do you turn it into successful implementation of an application. How can you ensure successful long-term adoption throughout your organization?

This booklet, *Building a Trusted Expert Culture: Six Pillars to CRM Success*, is designed to help answer those questions and to facilitate not just successful implementation but long-term adoption success. I believe true adoption is the aligning piece between vision and action. This booklet will guide you through the migration of your high-level vision into tactical, actionable steps that can be translated into a system. By spending a little time on the six pillars of practice outlined in the coming pages, you will ensure CRM adoption.

As you read, you will learn to engage and coach your teams to tap into the expertise in your organization, sharing information and ideas that will lead to real innovation and make you irreplaceable to customers. I'll share my observations and step by step instructions to ensure adoption across your company. I'll deal with issues of culture that need to be addressed before you begin and discuss the pillars that support CRM success.

To get the most out of Building a *Trusted Expert Culture,* interact with it. Jot down notes and thoughts. When you encounter a question, answer it. When you come across a chart, pause and fill it in. Your notes and answers will help you identify priorities and narrow down a starting point from which to begin moving toward a Trusted Expert culture. As you read, also bear in mind that these techniques apply to your entire organization not just your sales team.

The techniques and observations in this book are designed to be used and re-used as you assess and re-assess team development and customer care in your company. **While adoption of a customer relationship solution may seem daunting, *Building a Trusted Expert Culture: Six Pillars of CRM Success* will help you create a map to move forward.** It will help you gear adoption to your unique company, taking into account your particular strengths and challenges. Let's get started.

DRIVING FORCES—PERCEIVED

If you're reading this booklet, it's likely you're feeling the stresses of complexities in the market. You may have lost customers you thought were secure. Maybe you've had complaints about follow up or missed opportunities in AOR. You feel the pressure of indirect competition as it confuses your customers, pulling them in many directions. You're likely wondering how your team can adapt to the changing marketplace and how to collect critical information from customers.

You're not alone. Many companies are overwhelmed by the challenges of today's dynamic market, wondering how to get and keep customers. As pressure increases, organizations often decide the solution is to track everything and track it NOW. They see the need for accountability and efficiency and turn to CRM products to help them micromanage their employees and customers to gather data. **Facing lost sales opportunities and oversights, it is tempting to take this quick fix approach and hope a CRM system will repair what seems to be broken.**

In my experience, there are six primary issues that drive companies to CRM systems. If you're experiencing any one of these, it's likely you've thought about software as a possible solution.

↗ EFFICIENCY	↗ ACCOUNTABILITY
↗ COVERAGE	↗ PARTICIPATION
↗ PREDICTABILITY	↗ CUSTOMER LOYALTY

The first is **Efficiency**. It is often said that there are not enough hours in a day. Inevitably there are more tasks to accomplish than time in which to accomplish them. All too often people confuse efficiency with hurry, cramming every possible task into as little time as possible. Instead the trick is identifying which tasks are the right, most effective tasks.

Businesses purchase CRM hoping to find ways to streamline processes and create efficient procedures in order to cram in tasks when the real issue may be recognizing that they need to reassess the tasks to begin with.

Accountability is another common reason companies turn to CRM solutions. Lack of accountability leads to what strategic coach Dan Sullivan calls "open file syndrome." "Open file syndrome" occurs when tasks are assigned but management is left wondering if those tasks were completed. With no streamlined way for managers to track progress and note completion, assignments can get lost in the shuffle. How much time do you waste wondering if things have been done?

Coverage is another driving force to CRM. Often sales people are stretched thin and cannot cover all of the accounts that need attention. Customers begin to complain about lack of follow-up and unresolved issues. The damage to customer trust that results from these negative experiences is difficult to rebuild. It takes multiple positive interactions to restore lost customer trust.

Today's business are often at a loss to know how to identify customers who require dedicated attention and how to stay connected to all their customers whether or not they have a sales associate to dedicate to the account.

In the high-speed world of business, it can be difficult to keep up with the opportunities in your industry. **Participation** in your field is vital to success. It seems that the more bids you're in on, the better. To paraphrase a great sports quote by Wayne Gretzky, "You loose 100% of the deals you don't quote." As businesses miss opportunities and lost prospects pile up, they are driven to find a solution and turn to CRM.

- Complexity in daily operations leads to the next driving force, **Predictability.** Predictability can also be understood as repeatability. Companies are desperate to create some predictability in terms of forecasting and resource planning and are trying to find ways to make processes repeatable to minimize mistakes and oversights. As organizations add locations and are spread over large areas or even around the globe, the need for predictability and repeatability increases.

- The final driving force is a culmination of the rest. Finding ways to increase **Customer Loyalty** is the central reason companies believe they need CRM. Never before have customers had so many demands on their time and attention and inspiring loyalty in customers is increasingly difficult.

These driving forces are real problems that need to be addressed. Often the best way to find solutions to these issues is to create clarity around specific practices that are contributing them. In many cases, technology can help, but all too often, companies seek technology as the first and sole solution to these issues and find themselves mired in implementation problems. If you can first identify the problems you are trying to solve and then use technology to support those efforts, you will have a winning formula for adoption.

TRACKING TO FAIL

These six driving forces all seem to point to more oversight and tracking as the solution. Doesn't logic say that if details are slipping by, pay more attention to details? It seems to, and so companies do just that. They tighten tracking efforts and expect more from employees. While it seems logical, this response leads to a predictable cycle of implementation challenges.

Time and time again I've been asked to intervene in software implementations that are on the verge of failure, and almost every time, the process leading up to the crisis is the same:

There a few key reasons this process cannot effect positive, long-term change. The first problem is that the process is out of order. There is nothing wrong with technology solutions. Technology can and will help with your CRM needs. **But introducing technology before you know exactly what you need from it will not lead to success.** It is nearly impossible to successfully implement a product when you don't know what you want to do with it.

To accomplish implementation and then adoption, it is critical to have clearly defined results for which you are aiming, know what you want to accomplish, and create buy-in in your organization. A clear vision across your organization will allow you to select and/or implement a solution that aligns specifically with your desired results. You may start with manual or cultural changes—changes that can be made without a new technology system. In most cases, those changes will lead you to system solutions that directly address the needs you have identified and align perfectly with desired outcomes.

When you have chosen or tailored software based on its alignment with your vision, chances of successful adoption increase exponentially.

My first booklet *Trusted Expert Formation: Re-envisioning Your Approach to CRM* will help you identify and evaluate the issues that are most important to address. It will guide you through a process to craft a clear vision statement. It is worthwhile to go through the steps laid out in that booklet as you pursue a technology solution. If you already have technology in place, use the booklet as a tool to help you maximize the application by creating concise, achievable desired outcomes.

The second reason this process will not result in long-term adoption, is misplaced focus. The focus here is on functionality rather than impact. **While a software product with a lot of features may be attractive, it may not address the unique issues your company is facing.**

Jim Holst, a blogger for Cloud Sherpas, points out that companies commonly purchase CRM software based on the number of features it offers and then attempt to implement all of those features with little regard to the real needs of their company.[2]

You must identify the problems you are having and then identify potential strategies to directly address those problems. If one or two features greatly impact the issues you have identified, using just those will lead to greater success than forcing use of an entire application.

The third reason this process often stalls is lack of staff development. The obsessive attention to what has been missed in the past causes an anxious impulse to escalate oversight, increase contacts, and record everything, whittling CRM data down to its least valuable content—numbers. Companies over-emphasize numbers and quotas to the point that quantity is all that matters. Pressure to increase numbers can adversely affect your team's creativity and collaboration, which are necessary to innovation. **If your teams are filling up their time with quantity, there will be no room left for quality.**

As expectations increase, management tends to use the new system as a tool for reprimand—a "stick" with which to hit users. They look at the data only to see if quotas are being met and if sales people have made a certain number of contacts. Often staff members are encouraged to load everything into the system with no guidance as to what information is valuable or what the data will be used for. The data they load then becomes a way to track what *was* or *was not* done rather than a way to understand what *could* be done. It doesn't focus on potential but on failure, creating a culture of negative dysfunction rather than positive growth.

A dysfuctional company culture focuses on the past and what has been missed. A growth oriented culture focuses on the future and what can be accomplished. It recognizes progress and continues to press on. If a CRM tool is used merely as a means of surveillance and offers no clear benefit to the user, it will cause resentment for employees and frustration for management.

This is not to say that numbers and quantity don't matter at all. I only hope to point out that increasing tracking and contacts with no clear objectives will not improve outcomes. Only when contacts are clearly defined and the data they generate is used for the benefit of users and customers will they help your organization achieve growth.

When I come into these scenarios, it is clear that everyone is tired. They are worn out from having made changes in the hope of some progress only to find customer loyalty stagnant, team morale waning, and management frustration mounting. They are tired of what they have not working and too tired to fix it.

But the effort is not wasted. The instinct to track is not all wrong. There are ways to use a system to benefit your company, employees, and customers, but ultimately micromanagement does not provide what customers are looking for.

THE REAL DRIVING FORCE

The truth is, by focusing on increased organization and micromanagement, companies are addressing the symptoms but not the disease. I believe the real driving force, the disease that is causing symptoms in efficiency, accountability, coverage, participation, predictability, and loyalty, is dramatically changed customer behavior.

In their recent book, *The Challenger Sale: Taking Control of the Customer Conversation,* Matthew Dickson and Brent Adamson discuss these changes as they affect purchasing decisions and loyalty. In the past, buying behavior was driven by longstanding relationships. Without modern technology, customers depended on dealers and vendors for product and pricing information. They shopped directly and had little information outside of what vendors chose to share with them—not so today.

Today customers research price and product information online before they approach a vendor. They are bombarded with information and advertising. When customers do approach a vendor, more than 60% of the purchase decision is already made. **Less than 50% of their decision-making is based on products, services, or price. Over 50% is based on their experience with the vendor during the purchase process.** The result is that customers want more than products that work; they want solutions that work and insights that provide unique value.[3]

when customers approach a vendor
>60%
of the purchase decision is already made

products, services or price make up
<50%
of the customers' decision-making

>50%
is based on their experience with the vendor

Customers look for organizations that can provide distinct and valuable perspectives on their field and educate them on new issues and outcomes. They want someone to help them navigate alternatives and avoid potential pitfalls. If you can train your teams to anticipate the challenges customers face, help customers recognize those, and provide solutions, you organization will thrive in the complexities of today's market.

Customers return to organizations that make purchasing easy by anticipating and understanding their needs and challenges.

I recently passed an Apple store in my local mall and saw a line of people out front waiting to purchase the latest iPhone. They could have ordered it online and had it delivered to their door, but these people wanted the experience of having an Apple Expert guide them through their purchase, ensuring that they got the most out of their new device, and they were willing to wait for it.

Moreover, the emergence of the Apple Expert is an illustration of this trend in the market. Customers are willing to pay for expertise and experience when they won't necessarily pay more for a product. As products become more and more commoditized, that is, as it becomes harder to distinguish between products and price is the primary differentiator, customers look for companies that offer more in the form of expertise.

Another illustration of this trend came in my mail recently. AT&T sent a flyer advertising training to help me get the most out of my phone. They weren't offering a product. They didn't charge for this training (though it's likely there would have been some add on purchase options had I made the call). They were simply trying to retain customers by providing value in the form of expertise. Because cell service is commoditized—aside from price, it's basically the same regardless of which company you use—AT&T is aware that they have to offer more lest they get into a pricing war with their competitors and lose profit and/or customers.

These unequivocal changes in the market and customer behavior require reciprocal and corresponding changes in vendor approaches. While relationships, products, and pricing matter, they are no longer the primary drivers of buying behavior. Continuing to behave as if nothing has changed will cost you customers and profits.

Approaching CRM software as a silver bullet tracking tool misses the real problem. It attempts to address the issue in quantifiable terms—how many and how much. How many calls are made and how much data is recorded. Increased organization and micro-management, however, does not ultimately make you more valuable to your customers or help elevate your team's performance. If supplier provided insights have more impact on purchasing decisions than even products or services, how can you train your teams to create insights customers will find valuable?

Clearly, changes in the market and technology have remade today's customer. Realizing that the entire field of play has shifted can be unsettling but it can also be freeing. You can let go of traditional ideas about customers and begin to respond intuitively and effectively. It will take conscious effort and a shift in thinking but this booklet is here to guide that effort. In the coming pages, I'll define insight and detail sure ways to insight creation. I'll discuss priorities in choosing technology to support and train your teams in customer care and explain how to build a Trusted Expert culture in your organization, ensuring long-term adoption.

WHAT IS INSIGHT?

Companies that focus on insight creation are two times more likely to achieve preferred vendor status. They increase closure of forecasted sales by 24%, exceed expected quotas by 12%, and outperform competitors by four times.[4]

These results are certainly worth pursuing, but they are not easy to achieve. Building a company culture that prioritizes insight formation is a complex process. It requires attention and commitment. It is also hugely impactful, and I would argue, not optional based on current market shifts.

If insight is the one thing that customers are looking for in vendors, it is important to clearly define what true insight is. Let's start with what insight is NOT. Information is not insight. Remember customers can find information as easily as you can. Furthermore, while statics and data may be useful in drawing a customer's interest, they are not insight. True insight does more than inform. It inspires action.

When you know what a customer is accustomed to and what his/her assumptions are, you can generate insights and inspire action by analyzing oversights and misunderstandings that could lead to unanticipated problems. Often the customer is already experiencing problems related to such oversights and doesn't recognize the source of the problem. That's what you're looking for—the root cause of customers' problems, so that you can help draw the connection between their challenges and the assumptions that drive their practices.

The next step is to guide the customer through the obstacle you have uncovered to the solution by reframing the problem and helping him/her recognize the root cause so that the fix is clear and leads back to your organization as the solution. It goes without saying that unsettling a customer without also providing a solution will do little to create loyalty and trust. Therefore, insights not only challenge assumptions to create action but they lead the customer back to you as the supplier who is best able to help them act. Customers come to see you as a vital part of their operations as they rely on your insights into their business and your solutions to problems they face.

The insights you provide will make you the Trusted Experts your customers rely on, which inspires loyalty in a way that nothing else can. I believe acheiving this culture of expertise through insight creation should be the goal of any CRM implementation. I have come to refer to this process as Trusted Expert Formation and believe that shifting your focus from managing customers to teaching them, building a Trusted Expert culture, is the surest way to adoption success.

Customers want insights. Top producing companies create insights. There is a clear correlation between the two. When you stop micromanaging employees and customers out of anxiety and instead nurture an atmosphere that honors creativity and collaboration, you will meet customers' expectations.

CULTURAL BARRIERS TO EXPERT FORMATION

I was recently explaining the idea of providing expertise at a company where I was facilitating a customer care overhaul. One of the staff members said, "I find this whole thing really intimidating. I can't be an expert at everything."

It was a great comment. It allowed me to explain that true expertise is collective. You're trying to build a Trusted Expert culture. You don't need a bunch of individuals who are experts on everything. It would be impossible to train and maintain that level of expertise. But when you prioritize coaching and collaboration, encourage and enable sharing, you will tap into and pool the knowledge that already exists in your people and build an expert company. That is the goal.

A Trusted Expert culture is one that values collaboration to maximize expertise.

To truly address changed customer behavior you must also address company culture. Changing company culture is not easy. When people are used to doing things a certain way, it can be quite unsettling to suggest change. Addressing five key areas of culture, **acknowledgement, engagement, understanding, alignment, and measurement,** will increase success as you move forward. Your teams will be on board and energized, providing momentum rather than resisting and causing drag.

If these five cultural issues are not addressed, they can become barriers and derail CRM implementation. In this section, I'll draw your attention to these issues and help you create first steps to overcome them.

ACKNOWLEDGEMENT

Effective change often begins with acknowledging that there is room for improvement. It can be difficult to look at customer care in your company and see where it is underperforming. Processes that have been in place for years become second nature and can be hard to deconstruct even if you know they are not working. Remember a broken process is not a personal or business failure. Look at the process itself and allow yourself to honestly evaluate it without feeling a personal sense of failure. Sometimes it can help to bring in outside input to get a clear vision of what is happening.

Encouraging acknowledgement across your company will help you move effectively into change. People resist change unless they can identify and feel the disadvantages of continuing on the same path. Therefore, creating a clear picture of the problem for your teams will help you move forward into effective solutions.

ENGAGEMENT

Once you've acknowledged that changes should be made, engage your teams as you look for solutions. Create camaraderie and ownership by working with your teams toward desired changes rather than imposing them from the top. Engage people in the process from the beginning. Ask staff to help identify problems and give input regarding solutions. Involving them before you begin making changes lets your team know that you are working in their interests not just the company's.

The information you gather will help determine where to focus your attention as you move into creating a Trusted Expert culture. It will also foster a sense of ownership and loyalty among your teams and will increase the likelihood that they will embrace the changes that are implemented.

People often believe that adoption failure has to do with insufficient training. It is more likely due to insufficient engagement—imposing change from the top down rather than allowing your teams to help you create changes they are excited about and feel invested in.

UNDERSTANDING

Creating awareness of issues and then engaging your team will lead to a full understanding of the problem and its impact. Fully understanding where your organization is missing the mark regarding interactions with customers means you have clarified the impact the problem is having. Therefore, if you can identify negative impact—how an issue is affecting the organization—change is more likely. Create discomfort around a problem by drawing attention to it and then act toward change.

ALIGNMENT

When you act toward change, align action items with each team member. Assign tasks and behavior changes to each department and, more specifically, to each team member. Be very clear about each person's responsibility lest everyone think someone else is taking care of the problem and fail to act.

Change in company culture must happen at an individual level. The more concrete the task, the more likely it is each individual will engage and embrace the changes you are working to implement.

MEASUREMENT

Identifying a problem is the first step to creating a solution. The next step is measurement. Implement a solution and then measure it. Try not to overcomplicate measurement. Make success a simple yes or no. Did it work or not? If it did, great. Move on to the next problem. If it didn't, good to know. Try another solution.

Use the form on the following pages to develop actionable steps toward cultural change. In the first section of each of the following pages, jot down one of the top three things you perceive to be key customer care issues for your company. If you've read *Trusted Expert Formation: Re-envisioning Your Approach to CRM*, look at the obstacles to Trusted Expert Formation you identified and plug those in here as key issues. In the second section, think of the teams who do or could have a stake in addressing that issue. In the third, write down the negative impact that issue is having on employees and business. Then in the fourth, identify specific people and measurable changes they can make to begin resolving the issue. Lastly, write down what will indicate success or failure on this issue. Use these notes as a jumping off place to think through ways to create positive cultural transformation.

Remember, Trusted Expert Formation is not a technology system but a mindset, a culture, to encourage and develop throughout your organization. Address the cultural issues we've discussed and you will be well on your way to the changes that need to be made. Once you have done that and evaluated your overall approach, you will begin to see how a system can complement and support the desired outcomes you have identified.

↗ **ACKNOWLEDGE: KEY ISSUE** NO. 1

....
....
....

↗ **ENGAGE: TEAM INVOLVEMENT** NO. 1

....
....
....

↗ **UNDERSTAND: NEGATIVE IMPACT** NO. 1

....
....
....

↗ **ALIGN: WHO MAKES CHANGE?** NO. 1

....
....
....

↗ **MEASURE: IS IT WORKING?** NO. 1

....
....
....

ACKNOWLEDGE: KEY ISSUE   NO.2

....
....
....

ENGAGE: TEAM INVOLVEMENT   NO.2

....
....
....

UNDERSTAND: NEGATIVE IMPACT   NO.2

....
....
....

ALIGN: WHO MAKES CHANGE?   NO.2

....
....
....

MEASURE: IS IT WORKING?   NO.2

....
....
....

30.

↗ **ACKNOWLEDGE: KEY ISSUE** — NO. 3

....
....
....

↗ **ENGAGE: TEAM INVOLVEMENT** — NO. 3

....
....
....

↗ **UNDERSTAND: NEGATIVE IMPACT** — NO. 3

....
....
....

↗ **ALIGN: WHO MAKES CHANGE?** — NO. 3

....
....
....

↗ **MEASURE: IS IT WORKING?** — NO. 3

....
....
....

ADOPTION SUCCESS

Clearly, today's complex market has added new challenges to doing business. As companies deal with the repercussions of altered customer priorities and seek to improve efficiency, accountability, coverage, participation, and predictability to capture customer loyalty, they begin to wonder how they can retain all the seemingly important details. Often they get lost in tracking and numbers and lose sight of more effective, high-impact solutions.

Impactful changes are possible with the right focus. This section will introduce six elements of practice that can guide your attention and create that focus. When analyzed one by one, these pillars of adoption success will clarify your way forward and simplify your efforts to improve processes by making effective changes. Think of these pillars as working together to literally support your CRM efforts. As physical pillars depend upon each other to distribute the weight of a load so these pillars act as checks and balances of one another to keep your practices balanced. Top producing organizations use these pillars, and I've seen them consistently in successful implementations.

By looking at **allocation, planning, collection, collaboration, coaching, and innovation** in your organization, you will be able to see past tracking into real powerful transformations. These pillars are guideposts by which you can determine progress toward adoption success.

This section will explore each of these in detail so that you can think about your own approaches and needs. At the end of the section, you will find a chart to help you identify exactly what you need to accomplish in each of these areas. If you address these pillars as I suggest, using the chart to clearly formalize your desired results in each area, you will achieve adoption success.

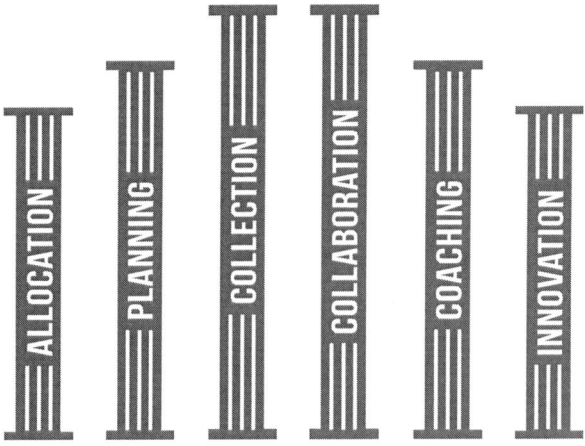

ALLOCATION

A system that will support your efforts toward Trusted Expert formation should make it easy to allocate and follow up on responsibilities. It should push targets and make progress easily measured and clear. Allocation can happen at many levels, from assigning customer contacts and classifying customers based on account priority to simple task management. Remember "open file syndrome"? Allocation, if properly supported, is the antidote to the open file.

> Customers are willing to release information to someone they believe can do something with it.

When allocating customer contacts, remember true customer care requires the attention of all departments in an organization. Customers are willing to release information to someone they believe can do something with it. Since this may not always be the sales department, allocate customer contacts to the appropriate department. Think broadly about contacts. Who in the organization should contact customers and when?

If you only approach customers when they are looking to buy, they will be guarded, thinking money and deal making. They will not be open about issues they are having or organizational struggles. Without that openness you will not glean information that will help you help the customer. Delegating contacts to departments outside of the sales team, provides the opportunity to talk with customers on a regular basis about a variety of issues. The information gathered during these regular conversations is rich and will move you toward insight creation.

> It's difficult to get a full picture of customers' needs if the sales force is their only point of contact with your business.

PLANNING

Allocation is a vital starting point but let me caution not to stop there. Move past allocation into planning.

In most companies, regular contact with customers occurs during the buying cycle. If the customer buys every 24 months, most contact happens in months 20–24. Unfortunately, this is the most ineffective time to talk with a customer since they will rarely discuss their needs and wants when buying. They are tight lipped and cost conscious. They have one goal—get it as cheaply as possible.

To avoid getting caught in this routine with customers, create account plans with a comprehensive approach to contacts that involve all departments and are particularly focused on creating connections outside of the buying cycle. It's difficult to get a full picture of customers' needs if the sales force is their only point of contact with your business.

You may think that this kind of planning will require more contacts and drain resources, but in fact, the exact opposite is true. Because customers have already made 60% of their buying decision before they approach a vendor, your focus should be on creating value rather than pushing products. Valuable insights will lead customers to your products and will close sales. Indeed, planning customer contacts can lead to a 50% reduction in the number of contacts to close a sale since strategic contacts create clear objectives and eliminate contacts with no goal or objective just to achieve a quota.

Customers need to know that you are working in their best interest not just trying to close a sale. If a customer believes whomever they are talking to can provide insight or help, they will be more likely to share information. Plan contacts accordingly. Who should contact the customer? When? Decide how often you need to revisit allocations and what needs to be assessed.

Contact planning can guard against common missteps that damage customer trust. Customers expect you to know their history with your organization—what they've purchased, what service contracts they have, when they need follow-up. Lack of knowledge or follow-up can damage a customer relationship and take years to repair. Taking the time to plan contacts and train your teams to prioritize value-building customer contacts will greatly decrease the likelihood that calls will be made in ignorance or that follow-up will be overlooked. Contacts will be effective.

Make planning a priority for which you have designated time. During planning sessions, allocate contacts to different departments depending on who can best meet the customer's need and provide or extract the right information. Put planning meetings on the calendar and dedicate at least one hour per week to each of the following—pipeline and forecast.

Your **pipeline** includes your entire customer base. Think about who needs to be contacted outside of the buying cycle to discuss business issues and goals. Every week there should be a plan to reach out to customers in the pipeline. These contacts must have an objective. Don't just call to call. Know what are you are going to teach the customer that they don't already know. What insight will you provide? Planning contacts with clear objectives will keep you from wasting customers' time with ineffective stop-ins and contacts.

Planning can also save time and resources by making visits based on location, knowing the proximity of customers to one another.

Your **forecast** is actual deals in progress moving toward closing but, for whatever reason, requiring further discussion or action. If issues are not addressed, deals in your forecast may unravel. It is vital to identify barriers to closing. What issues are still unsettled? Planning conversations in advance will help you proactively remove any obstacles in the way of closing, effectively minimizing the number of contacts to close a sale.

Planning is a vital part of customer care. It is proactive rather than reactive. Don't fall into the trap of thinking you don't have time to plan. In reality, you don't have time NOT to plan. **Weekly planning is one of biggest differentiators between average and great organizations.**

COLLECTION

Data collection to create customer profiles is perhaps the most basic goal of CRM. While it is basic, it is anything but simple. It can be very difficult to know how to capture rich data. Moreover, knowing what data is needed is just the first step. Actually capturing that data depends upon employees. True customer profiles include not just order history but detailed information drawn from conversations about customers' desires and challenges. It is up to your teams to draw out this quality information.

If you are dependent upon your teams to gather rich data about customers, how do you ensure that they will? It is vital to clearly define a customer contact, communicate exactly what you expect to be gleaned from contacts, and to explain how that data will be used. This section will help you identify whether or not you have done that.

I want to share a story that will highlight the challenges of data collection. Recently the general manager of a company I was consulting with, I'll call it Company A, called. He said his teams didn't want to load data in their new system. Moreover, his customer service associates and sales people couldn't agree on what to load. His managers had been on board during implementation but now their support was declining. They complained that they had to sift through too much information in the system. It was taking too much time and yielding little value.

> They recognized that customer contacts are not restricted to the sales department but occur everywhere, daily.

So I made a trip out there. I spent time with managers. They explained their quota expectations. Each team member was expected to make x number of contacts per week. Some did. Some didn't. Either way, there was little valuable data from those contacts. Reviewing the data felt like a waste of time.

I asked to see some of the call logs and sure enough, I struggled to find much usable data in the logs of contacts made by over 30 sales people. There was a lot of information on where people went—in other words, surveillance type data—but little that a manager could use to improve processes or provide perspectives for employees that would help them in that customer relationship.

I decided to ride along on customer contacts. Four or five calls into the ride-alongs, it was clear that they were right. Most of what was happening during those contacts was not worth recording. It was handshakes and stop-ins to be able to say the call had been made—quota met—that were ultimately of little value to the customer and to the company.

This is not a unique situation. It happens over and over again. Companies are upping the ante on their employees, requiring more and more, and then feeling frustrated that nothing is improving.

But this was a turning point for Company A. Company A needed to reevaluate not how many contacts they were making but how they were approaching those contacts and what was happening during them. Contact with customers needed to change fundamentally. They recognized that customer contacts are not restricted the to sales department but occur everywhere, daily. They also recognized that rather than focusing solely on quantity they needed to improve the quality of what happened during contacts so that contact would be more valuable for everyone.

Like those in Company A, employees resist collecting data when they don't see its value. They don't believe it is worth the time it takes. While time is the objection they verbalize, more often than not there are two underlying issues that more accurately describe their reluctance.

First, if your team resists data collection, it is likely contacts are not yielding valuable information. If contacts aren't yielding valuable information, it is because they are being made without specific objectives—quantity is being emphasized over quality and planning is being overlooked. If calls are made with a purpose rather than to meet a quota, contacts will turn into true conversations.

Contacts should create follow up—what's the next step? If team members are planning on a next step, they will be motivated to record the necessary information to execute that next step and help them the next time they contact that customer. Thus contact planning is vital to collecting rich data.
Second, data must be reciprocally beneficial to both management

and staff. When team members experience the benefits of data collection and data is used to coach them (more on coaching in the next section), they will begin building rich customer profiles. By building a complete picture of a customer's business, from current products and services offered to hopes for the future, you will be able to anticipate needs and meet them in a unique way.

I have spent a significant amount of time in the heavy equipment industry and one clear example in that industry of how intentional and detailed data collection can benefit you and your customers is trades. In an industry like this, every sales person can identify people who would buy from him/her if he/she had a desired traded product on hand. In addition, every sales person has active deals in which customers desire to trade components—products that could be gained through trade but are not currently listed in inventory. If sales people could identify desired products to gain through trade and match those to potential deals with a trade component, they would be more likely to close the deals dependent upon trade since that product will not sit in inventory but will move as a sale. The certainty of moving the product will allows more room in negotiations. Relying solely on the inventory at your stores limits sales. Having trade information in customers' profiles allows you to create solutions for them that go beyond products which will improve loyalty. This is just one example of how the right kind of data can benefit sales. Think about your own company and what data would benefit you.

The contact is the basis of any customer care process. Interestingly, though, I have found that in many companies the definition of a successful contact is completely unclear. If I ask five different people in any given company, from management to sales people to customer service associates, to define a successful customer contact, I will get five different answers. Everyone sees it differently. I've asked this question at dozens of companies and there is seldom an agreed upon definition. Until there is clarity about what should happen in a call, customer contacts will be haphazard at best. Therefore, increasing the amount of contacts will be much less effective than creating a clear expectation for contacts.

Like those at Company A, your teams need to know what should happen when they are in touch with a customer. What should be done before, during, and after? What is the entire process of a customer contact? When this is clear, team members will be alert for the kind of data you are hoping to gather.

I encourage you to take time to do this small exercise to help you draft a definition. Think of five people who have a stake in customer contacts. Ask them how they would define a customer contact. Use the space on the next page to fill in their answers.
When you've gathered this information, use it! Draw together

NAME:
ROLE/POSITION:

....
....
....
....
....
....
....
....

40.

NAME:
ROLE/POSITION:

2.

....
....
....
....
....
....
....
....

NAME:
ROLE/POSITION:

3.

....
....
....
....
....
....
....
....

NAME:

ROLE/POSITION:

4.

....
....
....
....
....
....
....
....
....

NAME:

ROLE/POSITION:

5.

....
....
....
....
....
....
....
....
....

ideas and create a cohesive definition. In two or three sentences, explain what a customer contact should be. What information should come from it? What should it accomplish? Yes, it has to be three or fewer sentence. If it's longer than that people can't digest it. Write a page long document if it helps but then hone it down to three sentences that layout the minimum requirements. It is important to be as specific as possible about what information should be collected and what will be done with it.

Definition: ....

....

....

....

Creating this definition may alter your thoughts on allocation and collection. Revisit those with this in mind and see how it impacts your process.

Once you finalize the definition share it with everyone—not just the sales department. Spread it to the entire organization and start to set the expectation that customer contacts are a whole company priority. Use it as a first step in training your teams. **This seemingly small exercise, defining what a customer contact should be in three or fewer sentences, will flush out a lot of issues**. As you continue through this book, feel free to come back to this definition and tweak it as you learn more about providing value for customers through contacts that truly teach them.

The most fundamental piece of customer care is the customer contact. While most companies recognize the importance of this piece of the puzzle, they focus primarily on increasing on the amount of contacts made. I challenge you to recognize that increasing numbers is just pushing more of the same. It is not changing your technique but merely heightening it and therefore does not address the real issue, changed customer behavior. You may see some percentage growth this way but not real exponential growth. But changing your approach to this aspect of customer care can create growth by multiples.

COLLABORATION

If you Google the word "collaboration," you'll get more than two million results. Collaboration has come to define how people strive to work together to meet the increasingly complex challenges of modern life.

Peter Diamandis writes, "Today, individuals and small teams can accomplish what only large corporations and governments could once do. Exponential technologies and the tools of collaboration are allowing each of us to transform industries and address humanities' grand challenges."[5]

This trend toward small expert collaboration is changing the way we approach problem solving and is sweeping into business.

In fact, today's most innovative companies are taking this small teams, collaborative approach and creating groundbreaking products and ideas. Even the biggest companies like Google, Lockheed Martin, and Nike are recreating small, start-up environments in the hopes of unleashing expertise in engaged and impassioned small groups and, by tapping that potential, realize exponential advancement.

Max Nisen writes in "Business Insider" about some of the most exciting and innovative work coming from these companies as they create places "where some of the world's most talented thinkers and engineers are given time and freedom to create something fascinating." In the 1940s, Lockheed Martin used this philosophy to create America's first jet fighter in just 143 days. Their highly secretive office of innovation is called Skunk Works and has become symbolic of the practice of freeing up employees to encourage innovation.[6]

Many companies have developed secret, small teams that spend their time coming up with the next big thing in their field. These teams are secret in part because they are encouraged to think so far outside the box that failure is inevitable. Some of the ideas they come up with never reach the public, but some, like Google Glass, will. Google has its own headquarters of secret, high innovation work called Google X. Other companies like Amazon, Apple, and even Nordstrom have similar offices that seek to free employees from normal, competitive, productivity pressures to increase collaboration and creativity.[7]

This approach is not only for the top innovators of our time. Any company can create environments that value and enable the expertise of staff and thereby set the stage for remarkable advancement. Collaboration is a key part of this movement toward innovation.

Indeed, globalization, complex economies, and rising demands of customers make enterprise collaboration essential for any business. In September 2013, Aberdeen Next-Generation Communications (NGC) released a study comparing businesses that prioritized collaboration to those who did not. The results are outlined in the chart below.[8]

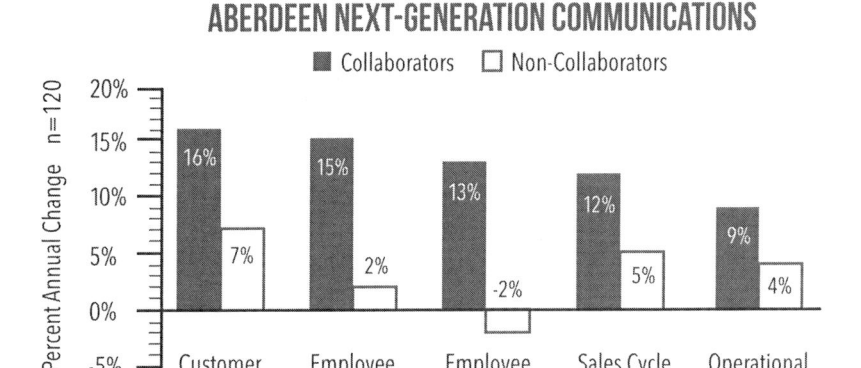

ABERDEEN NEXT-GENERATION COMMUNICATIONS

Percent Annual Change n=120

	Collaborators	Non-Collaborators
Customer Retention	16%	7%
Employee Productivity	15%	2%
Employee Satisfaction	13%	-2%
Sales Cycle Reduction	12%	5%
Operational Efficiency	9%	4%

Prioritizing enterprise collaboration improves employee morale, customer satisfaction, and efficiency in huge ways. It prevents knowledge loss and enables employees to make informed and empowered decisions as they find solutions for customers.

True collaboration within your company is more than hoping your teams are communicating. The Aberdeen study also found that "many of these business benefits do not happen for companies that take a laissez-faire or ad hoc approach to workplace collaboration." Rather, it's about having a plan in place so that "the *right* people connect with the *right* expertise or information at the *right* time to drive the *right* business decision."[9] Today's workforces are often separated geographically, so it is vital to find ways to keep them connected so that they can find information necessary to make decisions and help customers.

Too often, though, collaboration is hindered as data is scattered between various systems and is not easily accessible. Team members are recording and storing data with no easy way to share it across the organization. Communication requires a phone call or an email, at least one extra step. Often data is stored in various systems. Users have to log in to several different databases to gather the information they need. By addressing accessibility issues, you will enable your teams to find what they need quickly. The information will be available and in a format they can use to effectively address customer issues.

Technology has opened new possibilities for accessibility and collaboration. Customers expect your company to be responsive enough to deal with their issues from wherever you happen to be. Your teams need to be able to access and utilize data from any location. If they can't, delays can be a major inhibitor to data quality and customer satisfaction.

Imagine this, your team member meets with a key customer. During the meeting, he/she has real-time information about that customer's recent interactions with, say, the service department. The team member can speak intelligently about what happened and ask the customer if the issue is solved or if it needs further attention. Then he/she can record the customer's response and "tag" the service department if more follow up is needed, prompting immediate attention to the issue.

Rather than taking meeting notes on paper and waiting until he/she is back in the office, risking the loss of hard copies, the team member inputs notes on a hand-held device either during or immediately after the meeting. The notes are fresh and insight rich rather than flat and merely factual as they might have been with a delay. If that information can be shared across the organization in real-time, your teams will continually soak in customer information which will lead to insight creation.

When these accessibility issues are eliminated, collaboration becomes streamlined and is more likely to be the norm. A system that pushes information to people who need it and allows for comments and discussion keeps employees connected regardless of their location. Make data sharing as easy as possible. Remember, your teams will begin to see the value in recording data when they benefit from it as well. When data sharing is easy, collaboration is a natural byproduct of your system.

While technology will likely be the avenue to collaboration, your strategy should begin with your people. A clear understanding of the needs and behaviors of your teams will help you implement an enterprise collaboration system successfully. Pinpoint specific situations or questions that should be shared with others in the organization. Gain many perspectives to create valuable insights and solutions.

Remember, you do not need to have a company full of individual experts, but you do need to have an expert company. That can only be achieved through collaboration. If you tap in to the expertise that already exists within your organization, cultivating collaboration to come up with customer care strategies, you will begin to get a handle on today's market.

> While technology will likely be the avenue to collaboration, your stategy should begin with your people.

COACHING

Coaching is one of the most overlooked areas of the customer relationship process. As I noted previously, companies that are tracking everything to gain control of the customer relationship, tend to extract CRM data to use as a tool for surveillance—a "stick" with which to hit employees. Notice that this use of data focuses on the past, on what was or wasn't done. Instead, top producing organizations use data as a forward-looking tool to create coaching moments, help team members envision possibilities, and elevate their skills.

Coaching has been defined as "An ongoing and dynamic series of job-embedded interactions between a manager and his or her direct report designed to diagnose and correct or reinforce behaviors specific to that individual."[8] Note, coaching is ongoing. It isn't a static process, but changes over time as team members' skills and responsibilities develop.

Coaching is not training. Training is a one-time occurrence meant to transfer particular information. Coaching is a part of every day workflow and deals with actual and variable business situations. While training is about the acquisition of skills and knowledge, coaching is primarily about application—about doing rather than knowing. Coaching is also customized to the individual. It should take into account each team member's skills and specific situation and should deal with pertinent, pressing issues.

Indeed, if customer contacts and data are not used as opportunities to coach employees and help them gain deeper penetration into their accounts, team members tend to feel disillusioned with recording customer data. They may resent entering information that they believe is a waste of their time and energy. But, as we've noted, if they see data being used to increase their effectiveness, team members approach data collection with a desire for thoroughness.

Coaching is primarily about application—about doing rather than knowing.

It's helpful to think about data extraction and coaching in terms of social media. Just as Facebook is the perfect place to put out a broad request for information or an advertisement of some offered service so that you can tap all the connections and expertise within your network of acquaintances at once, so your system should give team members a simple way to draw on the knowledge, information, and expertise that exist within the company from a central source.

Facebook also provides value for the user in terms of information received. It is estimated that to keep users engaged, they must receive at least five pieces of information for every one they enter. This keeps them coming back and logging in over and over again.

The same is true of users of CRM software. If users are not receiving valuable information for every piece of information they enter, they will begin to feel like they are loading everything for someone else's benefit. This information doesn't have to be pushed by a system. It can come as verbal input from a manager, but feedback must occur.

While the coaching relationship between managers and employees is vital, it isn't the only way to think about coaching. Facilitate peer to peer coaching. Enable peers to review customer contact content and objectives together.

No one would go into a presentation without having reviewed content and practiced. Planning and practicing prior to delivering a presentation will make it far more appealing than a disorganized, ad-hoc approach. Likewise, peer to peer coaching facilitates successful contacts. If you can captivate a peer's attention with intended contact content, you will captivate the customer's attention as well. On the other hand, if the content puts the peer to sleep it will likely do the same to the customer. Peer coaching is a quick litmus test for whether or not you should spend time on that contact or reach out to another customer instead.

When I go into companies, I often ask managers what they think of the customer contacts their teams are making. I ask them if they would ask different questions or respond differently to customers. They all say yes but very few of them have ever articulated what they would do differently to their team. So I ask them to articulate it clearly. What would you say or do differently in customer contacts? Their answers are what they should be teaching their people.

Moreover, train staff to be assertive about gathering perspectives and culling knowledge from the rest of the organization so that their contacts truly provide value to the customer.

Anything you can do to enhance your teams' skills and improve the quality of contacts is direclty linked to providing the value that customers are looking for. Coaching is a significant commitment but it can transform your company's culture by generating an atmosphere of cooperation and progress that will provide a better experience for staff and customers. Indeed, one of the most effective ways to close more sales with less contacts is to improve your teams' skills in one call a week. Don't plan to discuss every contact, but always discuss the critical ones with teaching opportunities that can be used elsewhere. The lessons learned in this process will transcend into all other contacts.

Making this intentional effort to coach elevates the content and efficiency of customer contacts. When it comes to company culture, coaching does more to move you away from dysfunction to growth than any other activity.

INNOVATION

These pillars culminate in innovation. A Trusted Expert culture values collaboration and creativity in order to cultivate innovation. The better you understand your customers and your organization, the more you know what innovations you offer and what will make you valuable to customers.

Every organization has flexibility and creative ways to solve problems for customers, whether it's financing or key resources who have knowledge competitors don't. By paying deliberate attention to the previous pillars, you will uncover the innovations you already offer and see areas where new innovations are possible.

Think about what differentiates your business. Take the time to clearly articulate your organizational uniquenesses and make sure your teams know how to communicate those to customers.

Remember that changes in customer behavior have altered how business gets done. One major change that makes richness in customer communications hugely impactful is the current emphasis on consensus selling.

Consensus selling is the idea that more often than not sales involve multiple decision makers. In order to close any sale, you have to have all of these decision makers agree to purchase whatever you're selling and to purchase it from you. The challenge in these situations is finding ways to keep the sale from stalling due to lack of consensus among decision makers.

Knowing a customer well enough to identify key decision makers and then knowing what those decision makers are looking for and what will build consensus is the beginning of successful consensus selling.

Of course, assembling all these key decision makers at once in a meeting is the ideal way to begin to create consensus. This reduces the risk that one key person can derail a deal by missing the vision.

> Take the time to clearly articulate your organizational uniquensses and make sure your teams know how to communicate those to customers.

If you can't get everyone in a room together, Geoffrey James, contributing editor at Inc.com, writes that one way to move sales forward in a consensus sale situation is to identify decision makers and then to have several key conversations with those decision makers individually in which they make small but public commitments to your organization. These small commitments create momentum and the assumption that the customer will purchase from you.[11]

When you create innovative approaches through **allocation, planning, collection, collaboration, and coaching,** it is more likely you will close these challenging consensus sales. Your teams will be prepared and fully informed. They will know whom to contact and when. If they don't have a particular piece of information, they will know where to find it. They will know where the sale is in the pipeline and will be able to make informed decisions that provide innovative solutions for customers. This knowledge creates an irreplaceable team of Trusted Experts.

Now that we've looked at the top ways to address customer care in your company, how can you begin to move forward in each of these areas? On the following pages you will find a planning tool to help you think about what is most efficient and effective when implementing new strategies in each of these areas. I've provided a section for each of the pillars. In each section you will see an area labeled "Strategy." Use that space to begin thinking about ways to adapt that pillar to your use. Then identify the benefits of change. And, finally, clarify ways to measure success in each area.

The process you are putting in place is a cultural shift for your organization, which is not easy. These transformations will allow you to adapt to customer and market shifts.

Use this tool to help you define your goals and clarify steps to reaching them. Remember, it's important to articulate how you will measure these goals. You can't identify whether or not you have been successful if you can't measure. Though not every pillar needs to be utilized to get results, the more that you use, the more success you will see.

ALLOCATION:

Desired Results: Creating an efficient method to contact the right accounts and to increase market share and profitability.

STRATEGY:

....

....

BENEFIT/RESULT:

....

....

MEASURE:

....

....

PLANNING:

Desired Results: Create repeatable processes that teach your team how to consistently behave in ways that lead to success.

STRATEGY:

....

....

BENEFIT/RESULT:

....

....

MEASURE:

....

....

COLLECTION:

Desired Results: To collect the right information to make strategic decisions about how to provide customers with the most value.

STRATEGY:

....

....

BENEFIT/RESULT:

....

....

MEASURE:

....

....

SHARING:

Desired Results: Provide the best customer service possible, as efficiently as possible by utilizing the correct resources in the organization.

STRATEGY:

....

....

BENEFIT/RESULT:

....

....

MEASURE:

....

....

COACHING:

Desired Results: Develop your people and their skills within the organization to provide the most value to your customers.

STRATEGY:
....
....

BENEFIT/RESULT:
....
....

MEASURE:
....
....

INNOVATION:

Desired Results: Share new insights and solutions that your organization can uniquely provide better than the competition.

STRATEGY:
....
....

BENEFIT/RESULT:
....
....

MEASURE:
....
....

THE BOTTOM LINE

You may still be wondering, what's the bottom line? What is all this going to get me? Attention to these pillars will clarify the results you're trying to achieve. Without that clarity, your attempts at CRM implementation will be scattered at best. These steps will help you create balanced processes, create efficiency, and secure customer loyalty to protect your profits, your bottom line.

Here's how—as I've dealt with companies in the throws of CRM implementations, it has become clear to me that many of them are dealing with what I call the "iceberg affect." The largest part of their problem is not visible. They see the proverbial tip of the iceberg, and attempt to find solutions to those issues, but this is ineffective as it leaves all the underlying issues unaddressed and their businesses imbalanced and floundering.

Because closing and fulfilling/invoicing are closely correlated with profits many companies find themselves over-focused on these aspects of business—the tip of the iceberg. Their primary focus goes back and forth between drumming up contacts to create deals and fulfilling/invoicing those deals. Sales rise and fall depending on where the focus is at the time. When sales are high, they are focused on fulfilling orders and forget to keep the pipeline full. When sales start to dwindle, they begin to panic and drive contacts and other sale generating activities, only to neglect those activities again when sales rise.

This cycle is perfectly understandable. It pivots on sales. Businesses exist to create profit. If they are not profitable, they cease to exist. I'm not saying to ignore sales. What I'm suggesting is that there is a way to even out the ebb and flow and create a steady influx by creating efficiency that will lead to long-term, sustainable customer loyalty and growth.

The pillars provide balanced processes by which sales are ensured. When you address the pillars, your business will become proactive. You will pay attention to practices that sustain rather than inflate sales thereby ensuring profitability.

I see the iceberg a little like this:

INVOICED
PENDING SALE
REVENUE
ACCOUNT
QUOTE
OPPORTUNITY
ACTIVITY
PLANNING
VISION

Again, many organizations are quite focused when it comes to fulfillment and invoicing. They spend most of their energy there, on 10% of their organizational activity. The rest is underwater and a bit of a jumble. There is no clear process by which contacts are governed or opportunities are maximized. A guiding vision or goal doesn't come into play at all.

If instead you reverse this iceberg to create a funnel that is supported by the six pillars of CRM success and founded on your visions and goals, you create a process that leads to fulfillment and invoicing without those driving the action. This is a healthy, sustainable approach to business.

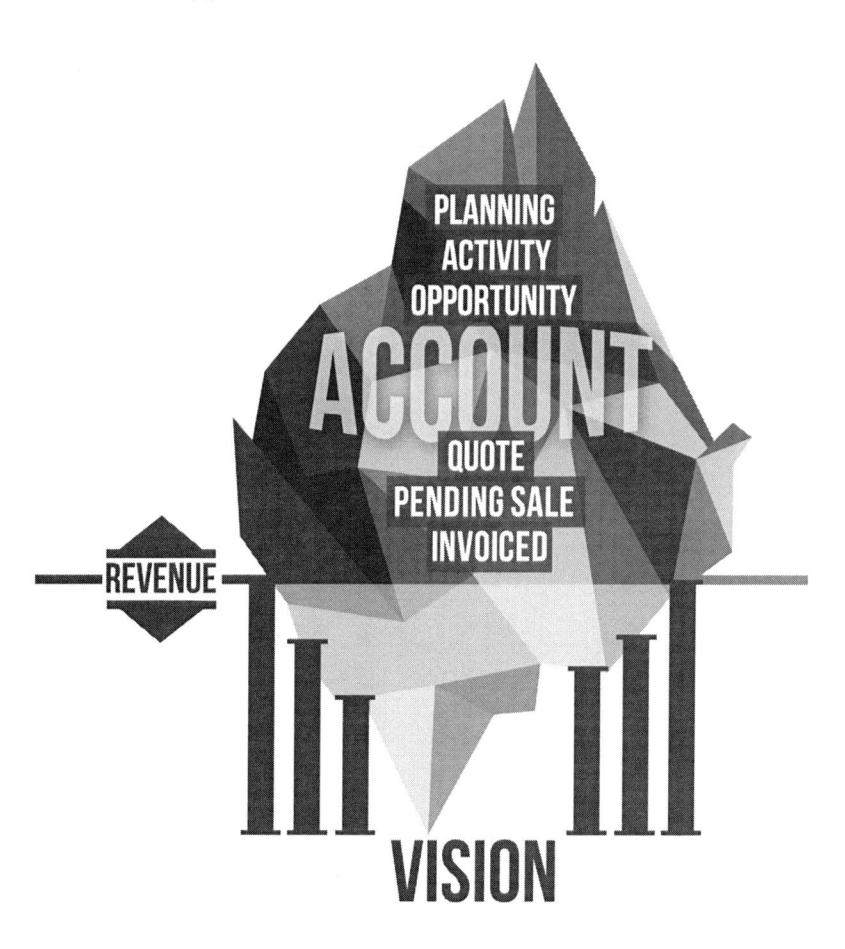

PLANNING
ACTIVITY
OPPORTUNITY
ACCOUNT
QUOTE
PENDING SALE
INVOICED

REVENUE

VISION

Companies want to achieve balance and find ways to sustain and protect their value. They are looking for best practices. They want to know how to transition ideas into an application. By discerning your desired result for each of the pillars above, you have begun creating rules to guide and balance your company's practice.

The steps in this booklet will lead you to CRM adoption success. Engage your teams and let them help drive efforts toward transformation. Look closely at your practices in each of the areas the pillars address. Are your efforts imbalanced? Let the six pillars give direction and balance. By spending just a little bit of time in each of these six areas, you will create real impactful changes that are actionable and measurable.

Don't be distracted by perceived driving forces. Focus on the real issues driving complexity in today's market—changed customer behavior and the demand for expertise. Let go of the impulse to micromanage and track everything. Invest in people—employees and customers. By elevating your teams' skills you will create innovations and capture customer loyalty.

[1] http://www.business-software.com/blog/cautionary-tales-and-tips-to-avoid-crm-implementation

[2] http://www.cloudsherpas.com/partner-salesforce/10-reasons-why-crm-adoption-fails-and-how-to-create-success/

[3] Dixon, Matthew and Brent Adamson. *The Challenger Sale: Taking Control of the Customer Conversation*. New York: Penguin, 2011. Print, Ebook.

[4] http://www.executiveboard.com/

[5] http://www.diamandis.com/introduction/driving-innovationbreakthroughs/45/#sthash.YLSV3TeQ.dpuf

[6] http://www.businessinsider.com/coolest-skunk-works-2013-2

[7] Ibid

[8] www.informationweek.com/it-leadership/why-enterprise-social-collaboration-means-business/d/d-id/1112149?

[9] Ibid

[10] http://www.executiveboard.com/

[11] http://www.inc.com/geoffrey-james/how-to-build-consensus-for-a-big-sale.html

NOTES:

62.

GORDON HILLEQUE

Gordon Hilleque is a graduate of the Entrepreneur Program at the University of Wisconsin, Eau Claire. In 1998, he founded Proactive Information Solutions and acted as owner and CEO. He is currently the owner of CustomerTRAX, a company he founded in 2002.

Gordon lives in Edina, Minnesota, with his wife, Emily Hilleque, and participates in his community as President of the Metropolis Foundation, which supports youth and amateur rugby through facilities and equipment. Besides being active in rugby, Gordon enjoys biking, skiing, and golf.